Enter the World of

Lathe-Turned Objects

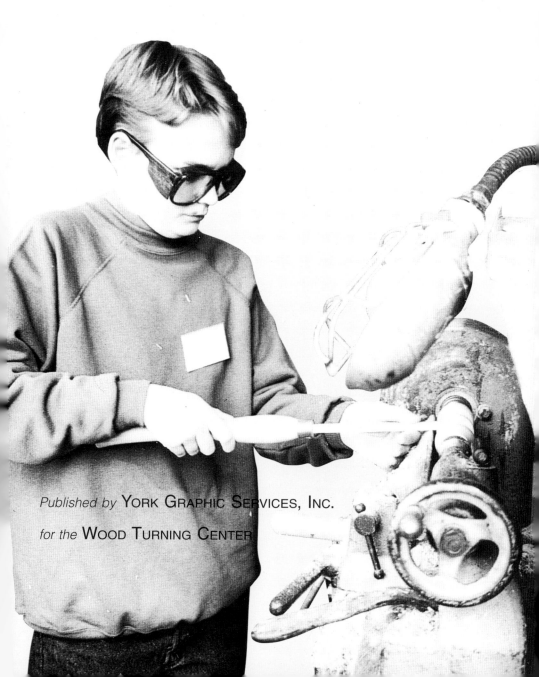

Published by YORK GRAPHIC SERVICES, INC.

for the WOOD TURNING CENTER

Credits

John Carlano, *photographer*
Judson Randall, *editor*
Susan Hagen, *contents*
Judy Gotwald, *contents*
Albert LeCoff, *contents*
Ray Chronister, *designer*

Photograph on Title Page

Boy, age 12, participating in Parent/Teacher/Student Workshop sponsored by the Wood Turning Center at the George School in March 1994.

Printed in the United States of America
by PrintTech, a division of
York Graphic Services, Inc.,
3600 West Market Street, York, Pennsylvania 17404

Distributed by the Wood Turning Center, P.O. Box 25706,
Philadelphia, Pennsylvania 19144

ISBN 0-9651966-1-5

In the spring of 1976, Albert LeCoff, a production wood worker with a desire to broaden his and others' understanding of the artistic potential of lathe-turned objects, organized a gathering: *Wood Turning Symposium: Philosophy and Practice.*

The symposium was held at the George School, a Quaker school in Bucks County, Pennsylvania. LeCoff was assisted by his brother, Alan, and by Palmer Sharpless, the George School's shop teacher and a noted production turner. Among the participants attending the initial wood turning conference was the late Jake Brubaker of Lancaster County, Pennsylvania. In order to commemorate the event, Brubaker gave LeCoff a vessel about the size of a softball called *Saffron Container with Tail.*

The symposium organizers didn't intend to start a wood turning collection, or even a wood turning center; however, an assemblage of objects grew out of the 1976 symposium and subsequent similar events. As Albert LeCoff put it, the collection started as a way of remembering these relationships and experiences with fellow wood turners.

"I liked them and I liked their work," LeCoff says. "Over the years, we continued to receive objects from artists and other donors even before we became an official non-profit organization. They gave the objects, sensing that they would be in good hands, and that an institution would eventually be formed to take care of these objects and promote lathe-turning." While the collection may only be seen by appointment at the present, the board and staff confidently expect that the Wood Turning Center's objects will soon be housed in a permanent facility for viewing by the public.

There were 10 symposia from 1976 through 1981. By 1981, what would become the Wood Turning Center had grown from nascency to maturity, and the happenstance donations of turned pieces numbered nearly four score.

At the same time, LeCoff became more deeply committed to a mission: to further an awareness and appreciation for lathe-turning and, in particular, to assemble a body of work representing the development of the field. Today, the Wood Turning Center's collection contains more than 300 objects. Through an active acquisition program, the Center has now become one of the most important collections of wood turning in the world. By means of outright purchases, donations and the unique adoption program, the collection has expanded annually to incorporate the most important examples of contemporary lathe-turned objects.

The collection, from which more than 160 objects are illustrated in this book, depicts the traditions and styles of objects produced on the lathe by turners from around the world. The works range from purely functional such as crafted door handles, to sculptural pieces that are sometimes whimsical, sometimes serious, yet always meaningful. Serious works, for example, might include Hap Sakwa's *Perfect Reflection* and Michelle Holzapfel's *Fishes Bottle Vase.* C.R. "Skip" Johnson takes a more comical stance, on the other hand, in his piece titled *Spud.*

Thematically, the objects in this book represent the contemporary evolution of this traditional art form. They show how many approaches there are to the use of the lathe and how materials are used as forms for their own sake or as elements to be re-assembled or cast in another form. For example, the objects in the Center's collection include an Appalachian chair with turned members, as well as a set of painted Russian nesting dolls. At the sculptural extreme is a large turned and chain-sawed piece by Mark Lindquist.

Appalachian Chair
H. 34 1/2" x W. 18 1/2" x D. 15 3/4"
Wood
c. 1800's
Loaned Anonymously
L96.11.15.001

Russian Nesting Dolls
Largest: H. 12" x Diam. 6 1/4", smallest: H. 3/4" x Diam. 5/16"
Basswood and paint
c. 1975
Loaned Anonymously
L95.01.01.199

Shaping objects on a lathe is similar to shaping on a potter's wheel, except that the rotation occurs horizontally and the materials can range from simple woods to metals to plastics. The lathe rotates the material and the turner shapes and carves it with a cutting tool resting on a firm parallel device. Unlike wheel throwing which can employ additive techniques, one major feature of turning is that when wood is removed from the piece it cannot be added again.

The Wood Turning Center is a non-profit membership organization dedicated to education, preservation and promotion of the art and craft of lathe-turning through organizing exhibitions, conferences and symposia. The Center's goal is to promote and encourage the work of established and developing artists and to cultivate among the general public and the art world a deeper appreciation of lathe-turning.

INTRODUCTION

The Center is devoted to preserving the history of lathe-turning through ongoing documentation of events and objects. Its archives are available to scholars and members for research purposes. Slides, books and tapes related to the study of lathe-turning are offered for sale. Objects from the Center's collection are frequently loaned to other museums and galleries. Recent projects include the traveling exhibition *Challenge V: International Lathe-Turned Objects,* featuring the work of 55 international artists and documented by a full-color catalogue.

The Center's quarterly publication, *Turning Points,* informs its readers about issues, activities and events occurring in and effecting the lathe-turning field from both a contemporary and historical perspective. The Wood Turning Center also organizes conferences, educational programs, panel discussions and lectures. The Center recently established the International Turning Exchange (ITE), a summer residency program for four lathe-turning artists, one scholar and a journalist from around the world.

Committed to furthering the creative development of the artist and the craftsperson, the Wood Turning Center offers a comprehensive membership program which invites all who practice or share an interest in lathe-turning to join and participate.

Jean-François Escoulen turning at the lathe during his 1996 International Turning Exchange residency at the George School.

The Wood Turning Center has grown from an ad hoc group of turning enthusiasts staging a weekend symposium to a globally recognized non-profit organization with a dedicated board of trustees and committees actively involved in community and international programs. We hope that this book will provide a useful and interesting introduction to an intriguing art form, where the craft continues to evolve.

BRUCE KAISER, *President*

Faceplate turning

Photo by Terry Martin, 1996 ITE Resident

P.A. ARENSKOV

California, U.S.A.
B. 1921

Orbicular

H. 4" x Diam. 16"
*Ash, padauk, purple heart, walnut, poplar,
bird's-eye maple, cedar, and red oak*
1988
Donated by Artist
G95.03.13.001

Peter Arenskov works with polychromatic turning. This is a
process where the artist first laminates different pieces of wood
to create a design, then the piece is turned on a lathe. The
theme of *Orbicular* is a swirling planetary configuration in space
reflecting various hues of colors from the sun's rays.

New Jersey, U.S.A.
B. 1916

Container
H. 7 1/4″ x Diam. 3 1/2″
*African blackwood finial,
apricot base, dogwood lid*
1993
Donated by Artist
G95.01.01.001

In this experimental container, Walter Balliet, a retired master machinist, used a pumping chuck with a swashplate attachment he constructed for his ornamental lathe. The decoration of the top portion of the base is the result of two reciprocations. The lower portion results from the action of a rose engine attachment. He uses these plates on many of the objects he currently produces.

BORIS BALLY

Pennsylvania, U.S.A.
B. 1961

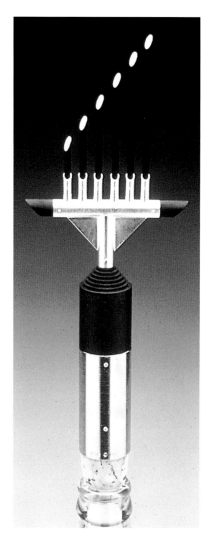

**Kalimba, Bottle Cork
Sculpture**
H. 8″ x D. 1″ x W. 3″
Silver, ebony, aluminum, goldplate
1989
Donated by Artist
G95.01.01.002

   A talented designer and craftsman with a BFA in metals,
Boris Bally designs and makes functional and sculptural
objects. *Kalimba, Bottle Cork Sculpture* is the first in a series of
bottleneck sculptures inspired by the African (Zaire) instrument
of the same name.

10

GOTTFRIED BOCKELMANN

Germany
B. 1930

Jar
H. 5 1/2" x W. 3 5/8" x D. 1 3/4"
Moor oak and amaranth
1988
95.01.01.006

Gottfried Bockelmann, a master turner and former head and founder of the turning department at the School of Art and Craft in Hildesheim, Germany, displays superb design ability and manipulation of the lathe in his work. Here he has designed and created an attractive jar in a unique oval form. The unusual combination of materials adds to the visual impact of this complex work.

11

Ed Bosley

Pennsylvania, U.S.A.
B. 1917

Vessel

H. 5 1/2" x Diam. 9 1/4"
Alabaster
1988
Loaned anonymously
L95.01.01.007

       Ed Bosley is a retired engineer who has explored many artistic media, including painting and sculpture. This piece is the result of his work with the lathe and alabaster. The form is reminiscent of thrown pottery forms. It is impossible to depict the exceedingly thin structure of this hollow stone vessel.

Pennsylvania, U.S.A.
B. 1950

Frog Bowl
H. 4" x Diam. 6"
Cherry
1988
Donated by Artist
G95.01.01.009

Michael Brolly's work is highly crafted, creative, and whimsical. He often creates imaginary figures through complex manipulation of wood on and off the lathe. In *Frog Bowl,* Brolly uses the bowl form as a metaphor—the bowl becomes a home for the frog.

JAKE BRUBAKER

Pennsylvania, U.S.A.
B. 1897   D. 1981

Saffron Container

H. 6" x Diam. 2 1/2"
Rosewood
1977
Loaned anonymously
L95.01.01.010

Saffron Container with Tail

H. 4 1/2" x Diam. 3"
Swedish birch
1978
Loaned anonymously
L95.01.01.011

      Jake Brubaker learned how to make saffron containers from his father and grandfather who were, in turn, influenced by Joseph Long Lehn, a noted Lancaster County turner. Brubaker was a toy pattern maker and Mennonite priest who turned first as a hobby and later as a full-time avocation. During the 1977 Wood Turning Center symposium Jake was challenged to produce something new. The following year he presented the Center with *Saffron Container with Tail,* the result of that challenge.

CHRISTIAN BURCHARD

Oregon, U.S.A.
B. 1955

Old Earth Series: Black Walnut with Black Fields

H. 5 1/2″ x Diam. 5 1/2″
Black walnut / ink
1995
Donated by Irv Lipton
G95.08.24.001

Christian Burchard brings together in his work a background in German furniture making and an education in sculpture in North America. In this piece, *Old Earth Series: Black Walnut with Black Fields,* he focused on creating a unified decorative object—not just a piece with superfluous surface decoration.

M. Dale Chase

California, U.S.A.
B. 1934

Lidded Container
H. 1 3/4" x Diam. 1 3/4"
African blackwood
1988
95.01.01.018

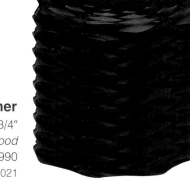

Lidded Container
H. 2 3/4" x Diam. 2 3/4"
African blackwood
c. 1990
95.01.01.021

Lidded Container
H. 2" x Diam. 1 3/4"
Ivory, African blackwood, and gold
1987
95.01.01.022

Dale Chase is a retired neurosurgeon who is now pursuing turning full-time. Chase draws on the rigors of technique and precision in medicine and applies them to the turning. He is one of a few artists in the turning field to utilize ornamental and rose engine turning, an avocation of noblemen in the 1800s.

16

M. DALE CHASE

California, U.S.A.
B. 1934

Lidded Container
H. 2 3/4″ x Diam. 3 1/4″
African blackwood
1989–90
95.01.01.015

MICHAEL CHINN

Washington, U.S.A.
B. 1950

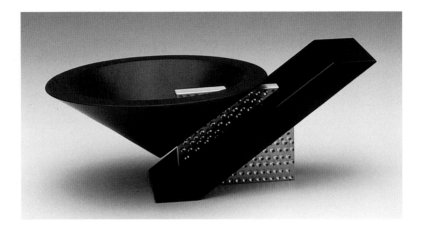

Tri-10,000

H. 1 3/4" x Diam. 11 3/4"
Purpleheart, Indian ebony, aluminum
1988
95.01.01.029

Michael Chinn's work has an unmistakable architectonic flavor. *Tri-10,000* is composed of a bowl form juxtaposed with other constructed, linear forms. Chinn has an MFA and a strong interest in 20th century architecture. He is currently a practicing artist and a professor of art.

Utah, U.S.A.
B. 1944

Nuts
Each approximately H. 1 3/4" x
Diam. 1 1/2"
Tagua nut
1988
95.01.01.030a.b.c.

Clead Christiansen, a production turner, utilizes tagua nut, a vegetable nut from South America once imported for the manufacture of buttons. His work exploits the beautiful textures and color of both the outer and inner nut.

PAUL CLARE

Wales
B. 1946

Bowl
H. 6" x Diam. 6 3/4"
Burl oak
1989
Anonymous Donor
A95.01.01.031

Paul Clare's pot evolved out of experiments with microwaving his work to distort gills on fungal forms. He also applied this method to tribal style pots, producing the effects of movement and tactility, as well as an ancient appearance. The patina was the result of "pickling" the object in iron salts and underlines the "oldness" of the work.

England
B. 1932

Box

H. 2 3/4" x Diam. 3"
Rosewood
1989
Donated by Artist
G95.01.01.032

Arthur Cummings used off-center turning to create this modernistic box. Cummings is a hobby turner who turns for the pure pleasure of making and giving his pieces away.

21

Frank E. Cummings III

California, U.S.A.
B. 1938

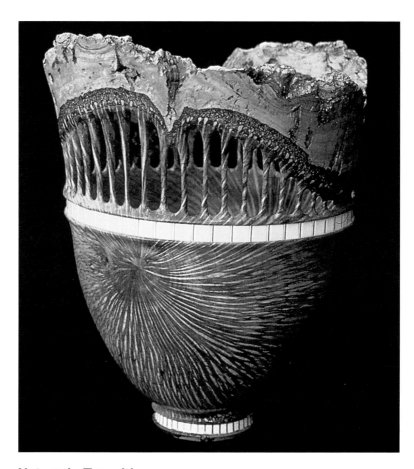

Nature in Transition

H. 6 1/4" x Diam. 5 3/4"
Cork oak, 18K gold, exotic material
1989
Donated by Irv Lipton
G95.01.01.033

Frank Cummings has an MFA and is an Associate Dean at California State University at Fullerton. Cummings brings a flair for the exotic to turning. This piece exploits and reveres the beauty of the grain structure of a full log, bark to pith. A rim of inset ivory and gold supports a series of wooden fret work, individually handcrafted.

Australia
B. 1943

Graffiti Bowl
H. 8″ x Diam. 13″
Wood, stainless steel, paint
1987
Promised gift by
Arthur & Jane Mason
P95.01.01.034

Mike Darlow, a production turner and noted writer and educator, makes whimsical statements with his turning. The graffiti on this piece makes lighthearted jabs at well-known turners and the field of turning in general.

RON DAVID

Canada
B. 1945

What to Do With Albert's
Toothpicks If One Has False Teeth

H. 4 1/2″ x Diam. 9″
Maytree, turned Japanese toothpicks
1993
Donated by Artist
G96.02.22.001

Ron David used a turned bowl sent to him by Michael Hosaluk. Hosaluk challenged him to create something from this turned form. David took turned Japanese toothpicks sent to him by the Wood Turning Center as a membership premium. The toothpicks reminded him of the porcupine quills Michael Hosaluk used on some of his vessels. This piece, *What to Do With Albert's Toothpicks If One Has False Teeth,* is the outcome.

England
B. 1924

African Hut Box
H. 1 1/2" x Diam. 2"
Boxwood
1989
Loaned anonymously
L95.01.01.035

Roger Davies is an internationally known authority on ornamental turning. He is a consultant to Christie's Auction House in England. Davies made this box while being videotaped to explain the process of ornamental turning. Davies turns for pleasure.

25

KARL DECKER

Germany
B. 1947

Door Handles

Left: L. 5″ x D. 2 3/4″ x Diam. 1 3/8″
Right: L. 5 3/4″ x D. 2 3/4″ x Diam. 1 3/8″
Palisander, ebony, rosewood, bone, brass
1987
95.01.01.036ab

Karl Decker has completed the official craft program of Germany under Professor Gottfried Bockelmann. He is a production turner. Environmentally conscious, Decker uses bone instead of ivory in these traditional door handles. The handle on the left is Decker's own design which uses a multi-axis approach to improve the comfort of the grip.

Australia
B. 1935

Bowl
H. 6 1/2" x Diam. 9"
Grass root
1989
Loaned anonymously
L95.01.01.038

Neil Derrington uses the root of grass wood to create a molten effect on the rim of this bowl. The work reverses nature in placing the roots at the top of the bowl. The effect is one of continuing growth.

27

JOHN DIAMOND-NIGH

Pennsylvania, U.S.A.
B. 1953

Untitled

H. 7 1/4″ x Diam. 8″
Birch
c. 1985
95.01.01.039

John Diamond-Nigh explores the bowl as a sculptural form. This bowl emerges from a wing form. The influence of David Pye can be seen in the hand fluting and the addition of texture to the turned surface.

Arizona, U.S.A.
B. 1943

Calligraphy Bowl

H. 5 3/4″ x Diam. 14 3/4″
Baltic birch, wenge, walnut
1991
95.01.01.043

Virginia Dotson's work is a unique departure from turned lamination standards set by Rude Osolnik in the 1960s and 70s. This classical form is constructed out of contrasting laminated patterns of Baltic birch and hardwoods. Her approach is painterly as opposed to Osolnik's decorative approach. Dotson has an MFA in woodworking.

Leo Doyle

California, U.S.A.
B. 1940

**Matched Candlesticks
with Matched Drawers**

Each H. 14″ x Diam. 4″
Bird's-eye maple
1987
Donated by Artist
G95.01.01.044a.b.

Leo Doyle is a professor of woodworking at California
State University, San Bernardino. The match-sized drawers
incorporated into these candlesticks are a prime example of his
ability to combine utilitarian function with folk or whimsical
accents.

New Mexico, U.S.A.
B. 1952

From the Wolf Series #1
H. 9" x W. 6" x D. 4"
Black and white airbrushed mahogany
1987
95.01.01.045

Addie Draper, who has accumulated solid credentials in woodworking and several other craft disciplines, has recently turned to painting. Her universal approach to the arts can be seen in this early transitional piece in which she uses the vessel form as a 3-dimensional canvas. She is steadily "breaking the surface" in her work as seen in the wing forms of this piece.

DAVID ELLSWORTH

Pennsylvania, U.S.A.
B. 1944

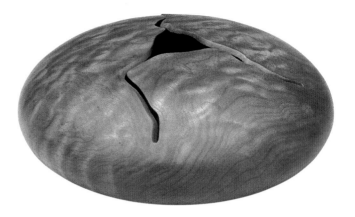

Bowl

H. 2 1/2″ x Diam. 7 1/4″
Quilted maple
1980
Loaned anonymously
L95.01.01.050

David Ellsworth has brought the art of hollow vessel turning to new levels, especially with regard to the lightness and thinness of the vessel walls. In the enclosed bowl form, Ellsworth shapes the opening as opposed to his more common technique of following a natural opening in the wood.

Pennsylvania, U.S.A.
B. 1944

Vessel
H. 7″ x Diam. 6″
Desert iron wood
1979
Loaned anonymously
L95.01.01.051

GLENN ELVIG

Minnesota, U.S.A.
B. 1953

Wait a Minute Dad

H. 36" x W. 56" x D. 20"
Lacquered mahogany, steel saw
1991
Donated by Artist
G95.01.01.054

     Glenn Elvig departs from his characteristic light-hearted subjects to create a statement about forest destruction. The saw is rendered useless by being cut in half. The turned wood piece represents the tree. Black was chosen to highlight the form rather than the detail.

France
B. 1956

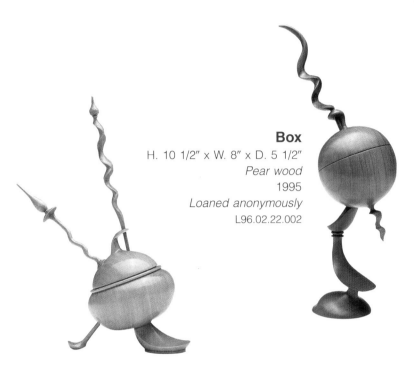

Box

H. 10 1/2" x W. 8" x D. 5 1/2"
Pear wood
1995
Loaned anonymously
L96.02.22.002

Box

H. 7 3/4" x W. 5" x D. 2 3/4"
Amarellio wood (Brazilian)
1995
Loaned anonymously
L96.02.22.003

Jean-François Escoulen is a master spindle turner trained by his father and accredited by the official French tradition of wood turning. These pieces were created with his own decentric chuck design which facilitates turning on different axes.

J. Paul Fennell

Arizona, U.S.A.
B. 1938

Miniature Goblets #3
H. from 7/16" to 1 1/2"
Tulipwood series
1987
Donated by Artist
G95.01.01.058

J. Paul Fennell turns miniature goblets with self-contained rings around the stems with masterful precision. Once a hobby, turning is now his full-time avocation.

Massachusetts, U.S.A.
B. 1948

Acer Quattro Aves
H. 3 7/8″ x Diam. 2 1/2″
*Various materials: Maple,
purple heart, padauk, black
dyed birch, spalted maple,
macassar ebony, zacahareus
nut, black leather dye*
1995
Donated by Artist
G95.09.01.007

This is the fifth in Al Francendese's series of *Totaro
Artifacts,* artifacts from an imaginary archeological dig. The
style and motifs follow those of the Celtic Druids of the first
millennium. Intertwined birds and a dragon represent friendship,
marriage, and peace.

DEWEY GARRETT

California, U.S.A.
B. 1947

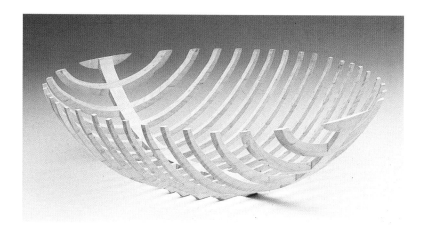

LIM #3

H. 4″ x Diam. 12″
Maple (bleached)
1992
Donated by Artist
G95.05.09.001

Dewey Garrett has found a way to expose the skeletal structure of turned objects. This work is stark yet possesses the flow and continuity of a solid form.

California, U.S.A.
B. 1915

Oval Box
H. 4" x W. 9 1/4" x D. 6 1/4"
Black walnut
1994
Donated by Artist
G96.04.08.001

Foster Giesmann focuses on both the design and process of oval turning. This piece, a combination of oval and ornamental work, is an example of this very difficult craft.

GILES GILSON

New York, U.S.A.
B. 1942

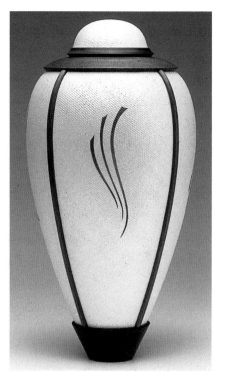

Fiberglass and Walnut Vase

H. 16" x Diam. 7 1/2"
Fiberglass and walnut
1987
Loaned anonymously
G95.01.01.063

Gum Metal Black Bowl Form

H. 5" x Diam. 11"
Mahogany, lacquer, flogging
1985
Donated by Irv Lipton
G95.01.01.064

Giles Gilson is a master of many crafts and skills. He combines multiple materials and processes to create both simple and complex forms. Top, a turned collar and base with a constructed wooden rib structure frame fiberglass panels. Gilson's exploration of the use of pearlescent paints and flocking has made him a pioneer in the revival of the painted turned form.

40

New York/Minnesota, U.S.A.
B. 1942   B. 1952

Vessel
H. 3 1/2" x Diam. 5 9/16"
Rosewood, holly, padauk
1981
Loaned anonymously
L95.01.01.065

Giles Gilson and Del Stubbs, in a rare collaboration, carefully combine different woods in an elegant shape which reflects the work of both artists.

The detail in the shoulder and foot is classic Del Stubbs, while the boldness of the belly and the contrasting juxtaposition of color and materials in the rim is a Gilson trademark.

Michael N. Graham

California, U.S.A.
B. 1943

Captured Sphere

H. 14″ x W. 11″ x D. 14″
Wood, lacquer
1990
Donated by Irv Lipton
G95.01.01.066

Michael Graham, furniture maker and sculptor, explores geometric forms. In this piece, he employs the sphere, cube, and cone to make a functional and contemporary coat rack. He uses contemporary finishes and materials to explore surface texture and creates tactile, as well as visual, art.

Michael N. Graham

California, U.S.A.
B. 1943

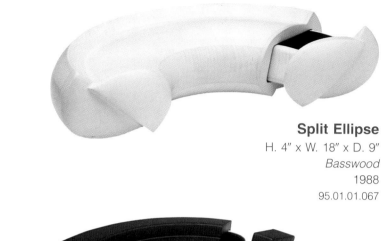

Split Ellipse
H. 4″ x W. 18″ x D. 9″
Basswood
1988
95.01.01.067

Circle/Square #15/35
H. 4 2/16″ x W. 9″ x L. 18″
Basswood, paint
1987
95.01.01.068

Michael Graham takes a different approach in a lathe-turned box with the fascinating movement of the curved drawer. Here, his interest in finishes spans the spectrum; the white bleached wood takes on the appearance of bone or ivory; the same wood painted black accentuates its form in a very different way.

43

STEVEN GRAY

Montana, U.S.A.
B. 1952

Parasol Kaleidoscope
H. 10 1/4" x L. 11 1/4" x D. 7"
Teak, ebony, glass, fused stained glass, mirrors
c. 1988
Loaned anonymously
L95.01.01.078

Steven Gray is a very popular kaleidoscope maker. He uses turned elements and forms in the construction of this stereoscope. The turned elements are structural, functional, and decorative.

Pennsylvania, U.S.A.
B. 1928

Ornament
L. 5 3/4" x Diam. 2 15/16"
Maple, rosewood
1987
95.01.01.079

Dave Hardy is a retired master machinist who currently shares his knowledge openly through classes taught in his own woodworking shop. Hardy displays his mastery of wood turning, construction, and design in this complex and elegant Christmas tree ornament.

45

England

Box
H. 3 1/4" x Diam. 8"
Yew and thuya burl
1989
Loaned anonymously
L95.01.01.080

Colin Haysom has created a highly precisioned, polychromatic, and classical form in this container. The combination of woods and a sensitivity to color add an unusual level of artistry to a traditional design.

Canada
B. 1942

Walnut Bowl of Walnut
H. 10 1/4″ x W. 5 1/4″ x D. 7 1/4″
Walnut and paint
1981
Loaned anonymously
L95.01.01.081

Bowl
H. 3 3/4″ x Diam. 7 3/4″
Mahogany
1978
Loaned anonymously
L95.01.01.082

Stephen Hogbin has taken a pattern maker's approach to turning. Here he has cut bowl forms in half and reglued them in different positions, finding the asymmetrical in the symmetrical. *Walnut Bowl of Walnut* has such monumental power that it could be the model for a large scale city sculpture.

47

MICHELLE HOLZAPFEL

Vermont, U.S.A.
B. 1951

Beet #2
H. 5 3/4″ x W. 7 3/4″ x L. 9 1/2″
Cherry burl beet with
yellow birch burl leaves
1983
Loaned anonymously
L95.01.01.085

Fishes Bottle Vase
H. 12″ x W. 14″ x D. 4 1/2″
Cherry burl
1987
95.01.01.086

As a sculptor, Michelle Holzapfel uses the lathe to quickly remove wood to a rough form. In *Fishes Bottle Vase,* a multi-axis approach combines two artistic objectives. She releases the fish from the "bowl" while creating "handles" for the vase.

Holzapfel's *Beet #2* again displays a unique use of the lathe as a sculptural tool. Her application of turning and carving in the leaves demonstrates a pivotal point that brought into conjunction her turning and sculptural skills. Both works display turning and carving used in sculptural harmony.

RICHARD HOOPER

Great Britain
B. 1958

Untitled

W. 16" x L. 15" x D. 16"
Birch plywood
1995
Donated by Artist
G95.09.01.002

Richard Hooper is an educator and sculptor. This piece explores the extrapolation of alternative forms from geometric forms, beginning with cones and pyramidic shapes. It is a sculptural study rather than a functional object.

ROBYN HORN

Arkansas, U.S.A.
B. 1951

Sheoake Geode

H. 7" x W. 8 1/4" x D. 6 3/4"
Sheoake
1987
Donated by Artist
G95.01.01.087

Robyn Horn, a student of sculpture and turning, was inspired by the work of Noguchi and the science of mineralogy. Her piece is a reflection on crystals encased in stone; a vision of sculptural form in natural objects.

Canada
B. 1954

Spectrum #3

H. 24″ x Diam. 18 1/2″
Colorcore, anodized aluminum, glass, lacquered maple
1986
Donated by Artist
G95.01.01.088

Michael Hosaluk's work incorporates the marriage of two areas of interest and expertise—furniture making and turning. *Spectrum #3* shows a sensitivity to contemporary design and materials.

51

MICHAEL HOSALUK

Canada
B. 1954

Tri-Cone
H. 5 1/2″ x Diam. 11″
Lacquered maple
1985
Donated by Artist
G95.01.01.090

Tri-Cone, a personal artistic breakthrough, combines the intricacies of a vessel form with the rigors of furniture design.

Australia
B. 1958

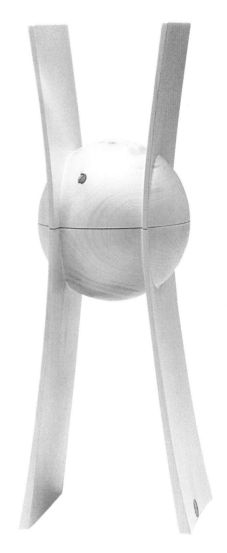

Vader Box #3
H. 15 1/4″ x W. 5 1/2″ x D. 5″
Huon pine
1995
Donated by Irv Lipton
G95.08.24.002

Stephen Hughes, a full-time teacher and woodworker, displays the influence of Stephen Hogbin's walking bowl series and Vic Wood's boxes to explore geometric forms within a sculptural container.

LYNNE HULL

Washington, U.S.A.
B. 1956

Basket #5
H. 8″ x Diam. 15″
Copper with chemical patina
1987
Loaned anonymously
L95.01.01.093

Vertical Basket #10E
H. 24″ x Diam. 11″
Copper with chemical patina
1992
95.01.01.092

Lynne Hull, metal spinner and teacher, has turned a vessel form, *Vertical Basket #10E,* into a dancing figurine. *Basket #5* depicts the burial ceremony of Southwest Native Americans. The vessel represents the earth opening to receive the spirit of the body resting overhead. Hull favors a green patina on her work to symbolize the Northwest ground moss now threatened by development.

54

Washington, U.S.A.
B. 1940

Tumble Pot #85
H. 7 1/2″ x Diam. 7 3/4″
Curly maple, cherry, ebony, aluminum
1994
Donated by Artist
G95.03.07.001

Jim Hume's *Tumble Pot #85* is an example of finely designed and executed stave construction, a type of polychromatic turning. Hume designs and engineers race cars and brings this precision to his work as a turner.

55

TED HUNTER

Canada
B. 1952

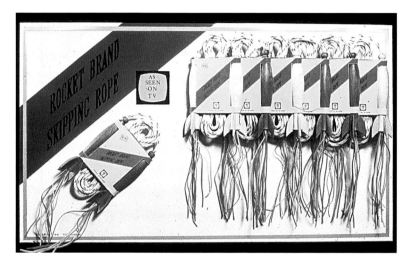

Our Children Watch

H. 17 1/4" x W. 30" x D. 4 1/2"
Mixed media
1990
Donated by Artist
G95.01.01.100

Ted Hunter, a sculptor and teacher, found the inspiration for this piece in his contemplation of the Gulf War. In *Our Children Watch,* he envisions a girl innocently skipping rope, but to his horror realizes that the handles to the jump rope are made from discarded rockets. This is a political statement on war and its aftermath.

California, U.S.A.
B. 1947

Rio Dunes
H. 17" x Diam. 11"
Cocobolo rosewood
1988
Donated by Irv Lipton
G95.01.01.101

William Hunter combines turning and carving to create this art nouveau style vase; one of the largest he has turned. Hunter is a veteran among contemporary turners. His work began with carving briar pipes, a skill which still influences his work.

C.R. "Skip" Johnson

Wisconsin, U.S.A.
B. 1928

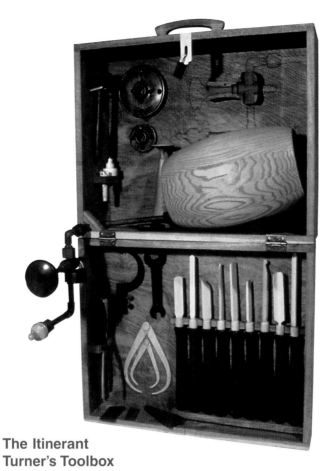

**The Itinerant
Turner's Toolbox**
Full-scale tools
Mahogany, basswood, walnut, padauk, honey locust
1981
Donated by Artist
G95.01.01.103

C.R. "Skip" Johnson imagines the life of a fictitious itinerant
turner. He creates a traveling toolbox/workshop to be hung above
the lathe. It includes all the necessary turning tools and a source
of liquid refreshment—a keg with a pipe fitting to allow the turner
to drink uninterrupted during his work. Johnson is a retired
professor of woodworking, now enjoying full-time woodworking.

Wisconsin, U.S.A.
B. 1928

Floor Walker
H. 29" x Diam. 21 3/4"
Cherry
1987
95.01.01.104

C.R. "Skip" Johnson's work is characteristically whimsical. *Floor Walker* actually appears to be creeping across the floor, an effect which is a tribute to Johnson's ability as a designer. *Spud, the Potato Peeler's Stool* (shown on the back cover), has an intentionally built-in squeak that can be heard when the piece is rolled across a room.

TOBIAS KAYE

England
B. 1956

Sounding Bowl

H. 5 1/2″ x Diam. 15″
Cherry, rosewood, bronze wound steel strings
1987
Loaned anonymously
L95.01.01.107

Tobias Kaye turns the vessel into a musical instrument. His pieces have become popular with professional music therapists due to the combination of visual and audio elements. Formally, there is an exquisite tension between the lines of the strings and the curvature of the bowl.

60

England
B. 1958

Three Tray Hinged, No. 649
H. 4" x Diam. 2"
African blackwood, boxwood, nickel silver hinge
1987
95.01.01.110

Richard Kell is a self-taught master machinist and designer who makes fine measuring tools. His skill as a designer and craftsman can be seen in this traveling jewelry case which incorporates turned components and a machine inlaid sterling silver hinge. When the case is opened, a perfectly nested set of containers is revealed.

61

DON KELLY

Massachusetts, U.S.A.
B. 1949

Walnut Bowl

H. 7 1/2" x Diam. 6 1/4"
Walnut
1981
Loaned anonymously
L95.01.01.114

Don Kelly explores the manipulation of material on the lathe and challenges the meaning and utilization of the bowl form. His work also addresses issues of scale and perception.

California, U.S.A.
B. 1953

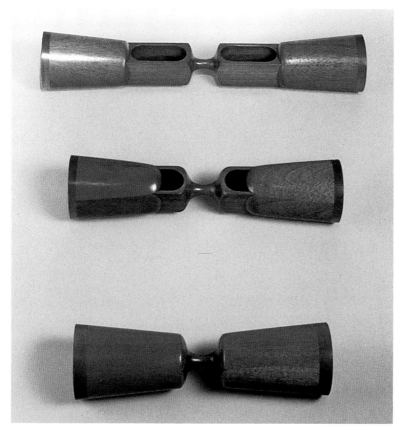

Box
L. 10 1/2″ x Diam. 3″
Mahogany
1988
Loaned anonymously
L95.01.01.116

Aspy Khambatta makes both one-of-a-kind and production furniture. His approach to design is influenced by his teacher, Leo Doyle. This cleverly designed and executed interlocking box has two concealed compartments.

FRANK KNOX

New York, U.S.A.
B. 1902   D. 1990

Lidded Container

H. 5 1/2" x Diam. 7 5/8"
*Big leaf maple, pink ivory
wood, silver pine stump,
redwood, African blackwood*
c. 1980
Loaned anonymously
L95.01.01.117

Frank Knox developed many patterns from his experimentation with the Holtzapffel lathe. The design of the box lid on *Lidded Container* was originally planned to be extremely complex, but recognizing the beauty of the wood, Knox simplified his plans. Both the design and the wood benefit from the compromise. A similar balance between complex surface decoration and beauty of material can be seen in *Compote Bowl*.

New York, U.S.A.
B. 1902   D. 1990

Compote Bowl

H. 9 1/2″ x Diam. 7″
Bowl & Stem: California Clara walnut
Base: unidentified wood on Incienso
1976
Loaned anonymously
L95.01.01.119

Candlesticks

H. 11 1/4″
Lignum vitae, blackwood, Corian
1987
95.01.01.118a.b

Frank Knox revived the centuries-old art form of ornamental turning, adding a contemporary design sensibility. He began pursuing woodworking after retiring. His work was primarily ornamental because he learned to turn on the Holtzapffel lathe. These candlesticks combine exotic woods and the contemporary material Corian, a man-made substitute for ivory.

Michael Korhun

New York, U.S.A.
B. 1924

Plate

Diam. 16 7/8" x H. 3/4"
Padauk, silver
1992
Donated by Irv Lipton & Artist
G95.01.01.120

Star

Diam. 7" x W. 3/4"
Box elder, black walnut,
padauk, golden beads
1995
Donated by Artist
G95.09.01.006.d

Christmas Tree Ornaments

Egg	Angel	Bell
H. 4" x Diam. 2 3/4"	H. 6 1/2" x W. 3 1/2"	H. 4 1/2" x Diam. 3 1/2"
Box elder	*Box elder, inlaid with beads*	*Box elder*
1995	1995	1995
Donated by Artist	*Donated by Artist*	*Donated by Artist*
G95.09.01.006.c	G95.09.01.006.a	G95.09.01.006.b

Michael Korhun makes exquisitely designed and crafted objects which require a high level of skill. His genius lies in the reinterpretation of traditional Ukrainian decorative art in contemporary American terms.

California, U.S.A.
B. 1946

Lidded Vessel
H. 6 1/2″ x Diam. 6 9/16″
Spalted tiger-striped myrtle
1988
Donated by Artist
G95.01.01.121

"R.W." Bob Krauss specializes in making boxes. A student of the history of containers, Krauss has been influenced by Del Stubbs' contemporary boxes. In turn, Stubbs greatly respects Krauss's achievements. This box, *Lidded Vessel*, displays a superb sense of design and craftsmanship.

67

Colorado, U.S.A.
B. 1948

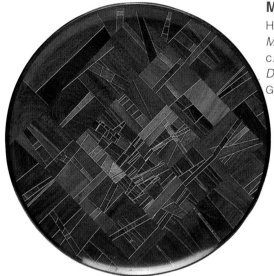

Magahomapleny, Bowl #46

H. 2 1/2″ x Diam. 24″
Mahogany, maple, imbuya
c. 1987
Donated by Artist
G95.01.01.123

Alabaster Vessel #79

H. 6″ x Diam. 8 1/8″
Colorado alabaster, ebony and
eatine (bloodwood)
1987
Donated by Artist
G95.01.01.124

Max Krimmel explores polychromatic turning and the use of alabaster. *Magahomapleny, Bowl #46* depicts random chaos created from exotic scraps from his guitar-building business. The name "Magahomapleny" is derived from *mahogany* and *maple,* all mixed-up and reassembled. The *Alabaster Vessel #79* is an early piece that incorporates a step in the rim which was an original part of the stone. The artist originally disliked the natural step, but now regards it as serendipitous.

North Carolina, U.S.A.
B. 1951

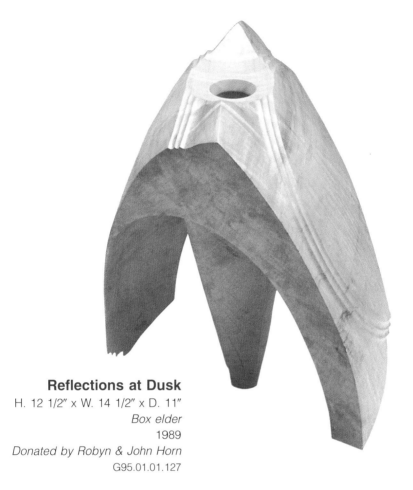

Reflections at Dusk
H. 12 1/2" x W. 14 1/2" x D. 11"
Box elder
1989
Donated by Robyn & John Horn
G95.01.01.127

Stoney Lamar has explored aspects of the turned vessel form over much of his career as an artist. Recently, he has moved away from the vessel and embraced pure sculpture, exploring the themes of geometry, architecture, and the self-portrait. *Reflections at Dusk* freezes a moment in Lamar's transition from vessel to sculpture.

Bud Latven

New Mexico, U.S.A.
B. 1949

Blue Stain Vase Series #2

H. 6 1/2″ x Diam. 5″
Wood, maple, ebony, veneers
1986
Loaned anonymously
L95.01.01.130

Bud Latven explores polychromatic turning of vessel forms. In *Blue Stain Vase Series #2,* Latven's vessel can be seen as a constructed curvilinear canvas which utilizes color through bleaching and staining of the surface. Images of ghost-like figures float around the circumference of the vessel.

California, U.S.A.
B. 1942

Jewelry Box
H. 7″ x W. 16″ x D. 6″
Bird's-eye maple, andaman, Brazilian rosewood, padauk
1988
Donated by Artist
G95.01.01.132

Robert Leung holds a degree in woodworking and was influenced by his teacher Leo Doyle. He designs unique furniture and containers. *Jewelry Box* has hidden compartments for jewelry and a lid that ingeniously reverses to reveal a hidden mirror.

Mark Lindquist

Florida, U.S.A.
B. 1949

Drum Song #1
H. 23" x Diam. 16 1/2"
Walnut
1987
Loaned anonymously
L95.01.01.137

In *Drum Song #1,* Mark Lindquist begins with the breakaway point left by the sawyer in the wood. Lindquist uses the traditional elements of spindle turning: starting with the foot and pedestal, rising to the shoulder and rim. He adds unique textures that are both hand-carved and created by machines.

Florida, U.S.A.
B. 1949

Spalted Maple Bowl, Carved Foot
H. 4 1/2″ x Diam. 10″
Spalted maple
1977
Promised gift by
Arthur & Jane Mason
P95.01.01.136

Mark Lindquist's bowl form with five individually carved feet pushes the art of bowl crafting beyond the traditional. His experience with ceramics is revealed by the manner in which the bowl rises from its base. The base is an important part of the design and an integral compositional feature.

MEL LINDQUIST

Florida, U.S.A.
B. 1911

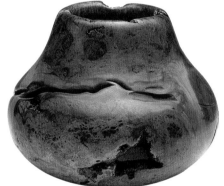

Spalted Elm Vase—Hollow

H. 8" x Diam. 6 1/2"
Spalted elm
1980
Loaned anonymously
L95.01.01.134

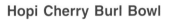

Hopi Cherry Burl Bowl

H. 8 1/4" x Diam. 12 3/4"
Cherry burl
1986
Donated by Ron Wornick
G95.01.01.135

Mel Lindquist, a pioneer in contemporary turning, uses burl and spalted wood in thick-walled hollow vessel forms. *Hopi Cherry Burl Bowl* is a classic example of his series of bowls which were influenced by Hopi ceramic bowls. *Spalted Elm Vase* is the first in his exploration of geometric elements in the vase form.

New York, U.S.A.
B. 1949

Post-Melvin Bud-Bowl #2
H. 11 1/2" x W. 8" x D. 9"
Spalted elm stump, spalted dogwood, and walnut
January 1986
Loaned anonymously
L95.01.01.138

Steve Loar, a professor of art and design and a Dean at Rochester Institute of Technology, usually sketches, plans, and paints his work in turning. However, he created *Post-Melvin Bud-Bowl #2* spontaneously, with no sketching or planning. The stump/base was initially cut at ground level. The open slot was a creative response to a small crack that was there. Loar claims that the piece was a direct response to Mel Lindquist's bud vases.

JACK MANKIEWICZ

West Germany
B. 1947

Fountain Pen
L. 5 1/2″ x Diam. 1/2″
Snakewood, ebony, burr oak
1987
95.01.01.139

Jack Mankiewicz completed a master program under Professor Gottfried Bockelmann. *Fountain Pen* is one of his many finely designed and executed production items. The design uses different color woods and finely turned inset brass collars and mechanics.

England

Plate
H. 2" x Diam. 12 1/4"
Maple, paint, scorched
1987
Loaned anonymously
L95.01.01.141

Guy Martin, a furniture maker and turner, displays his unique surface treatment of scorching and painting to create this three-dimensional canvas. The scorching creates a boundary for flowing paint and becomes a design element in its own right.

JOHN MEGIN

Pennsylvania, U.S.A.
B. 1948   D. 1986

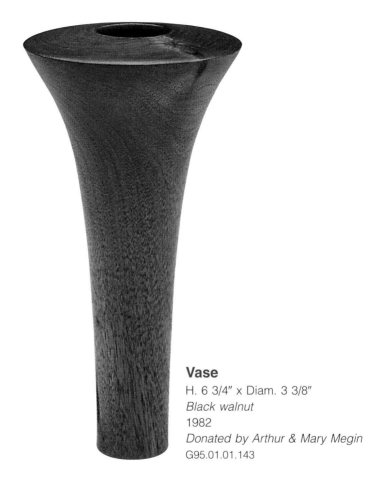

Vase
H. 6 3/4" x Diam. 3 3/8"
Black walnut
1982
Donated by Arthur & Mary Megin
G95.01.01.143

John Megin's work in vessels resulted in this unique inverted volcano form. Megin began turning traditional hollow vessel forms. With this piece he moved to a more sculptural form. His exploration of this new horizon was cut short by his death in 1986.

Vermont, U.S.A.
B. 1945

Hat
H. 5″ x Diam. 15″
Black cherry
1990
Donated by Artist
G95.01.01.148

Johannes Michelsen creates the perfect accessory for the wood turner—the wooden hat. Inspired by Albert and Tina LeCoff's country-western wedding, he worked from an idea he had contemplated for many years. After making this first hat, Michelsen has gone on to refine "hat turning" in many styles and sizes.

BRUCE MITCHELL

California, U.S.A.
B. 1949

Hydra Series #3
H. 13 5/8" x W. 15 1/4"
California walnut burl
1987
Promised gift by Don Roy King
P95.01.01.150

Bruce Mitchell, combining skills in both turning and sculpting, honors the natural beauty and flaws of the material in his piece *Hydra Series #3*. Mitchell does not attempt to conceal nature's "flaws." On the contrary, he strives to emphasize them with gestures made with a chainsaw. Man and nature are collaborators in this work of art.

Vermont, U.S.A.
B. 1946

**Lidded Vessel with
Natural Top**

H. 5″ x Diam. 4 1/2″
Spalted elm burl with walnut
1987
95.01.01.151

Michael Mode's work begins with the natural world of wood in a tree and ends with the human world of beautiful and useful objects in the home. In this piece the natural surface of the lid clearly reminds us of the "tree-ness" of the material.

GAEL MONTGOMERIE

New Zealand
B. 1949

Bowl
H. 7 1/2" x Diam. 11 1/2"
Maple, paint
1990
95.01.01.157

Gael Montgomerie brings artistic harmony to this piece by combining the arts of turning, painting, and weaving. Her design unites the diverse elements seamlessly. The inner bowl is starkly white. The outer bowl resembles an impressionist's work. The rim reminds the viewer that the piece is of wood.

Oregon, U.S.A.
B. 1945

Timna
H. 10 1/4″ x Diam. 11 3/8″
Wood and metal: Madrone burl and spun copper
1990
95.01.01.158

William Moore's *Timna* was the first in a series of four pieces which explored stacking multiple spun metal or turned wood forms to create a single vessel. This vessel consists of both turned wood elements and spun copper elements to create a geometric form.

83

Dennis Mueller

Pennsylvania, U.S.A.
B. 1951

Viper

H. 18 3/4″ x W. 15″ x Diam. 12″
Bleached ash
1990
Loaned anonymously
L95.01.01.159

In *Viper* Dennis Mueller turned two separate pieces
and then combined them into a single sculptural object. It is
cantilevered and stands upright, seeming to defy gravity.
Carving on all of the machined surfaces further accentuates
the reptilian appearance of the sculptural object.

LIZ AND MICHAEL O'DONNELL

Scotland

B. 1944   B. 1942

Bird Bowl
H. 6" x Diam. 17 1/2"
European beech and oil paints
1990
Donated by Artists
G95.01.01.160

The O'Donnells, Liz a painter and Michael a wood turner, collaborated to create *Bird Bowl*. The painted bowl is a nest for turned eggs, while painted birds peer over the rim. Michael is a production turner, teacher, and sheep farmer who writes and travels extensively. His early work was in bowls, with Liz adding cut bird forms. Their collaboration has evolved into pure painting on a surface turned precisely for that purpose.

LIAM O'NEILL

Ireland
B. 1949

Bog Oak Bowl
H. 1 1/2″ x D. 6 3/4″ x W. 9 1/2″
5,000-year-old wood
1985
Loaned anonymously
L95.01.01.163

Liam O'Neill created *Bog Oak Bowl* from a 5,000-year-old tree found in a bog. He turned the wood immediately on discovery into a perfect round shape. Within a day the piece naturally distorted into its present oval, ripplying form. O'Neill is a production turner and teacher who travels to promote lathe-turning.

Kentucky, U.S.A.
B. 1915

Candlesticks
H. 9 1/2" x Diam. 2 3/8",
H. 8 3/4" x Diam. 2 3/8",
H. 7 1/4" x Diam. 2 3/8"
Walnut
1987
Loaned anonymously
L95.01.01.164

Rolling Pin
L. 18 3/4" x Diam. 2 1/2"
Birch plywood, walnut, rosewood
1977
Loaned anonymously
L95.01.01.165

Rude Osolnik, a pioneer in turning, is an educator and turner who produces production and one-of-a-kind pieces. His impressive collection of candlesticks has been winning awards for decades. The rolling pin combines functionality and artistic vision.

Rude Osolnik

Kentucky, U.S.A.
B. 1915

Bowl
H. 11" x Diam. 8 1/2"
Birch plywood,
walnut veneer
1977
Loaned anonymously
L95.01.01.166

Bowl
H. 1 3/16" x W. 6" x D. 6"
Maple impregnated
with colored plastic
1966
Loaned anonymously
L95.01.01.167

Revolutionary for its time, in the top bowl Rude Osolnik combines birch plywood and walnut veneer in a functional and decorative manner. The pattern, which evolved from the turning process, is carefully conceived and beautiful. In the second bowl, Osolnik used plastic impregnated scrap wood from a veneer mill. The bowl rim is defined by the natural edge of the discarded log. Osolnik used recycled materials for years before it became fashionable.

England
B. 1953

Blood Vessel Series

H. 6″ x L. 10 1/4″ x D. 7 1/2″
Scorched burr oak
1987
Loaned anonymously
L95.01.01.170

Blood Vessel Series

H. 2 3/4″ x Diam. 3″
Scorched oak and baby powder
1987
Loaned anonymously
L95.01.01.171

Jim Partridge's *Blood Vessel Series* explores the emerging bowl form with a medieval sensibility. The scorching technique he employs on the surface gives the bowl an ancient appearance. Unmistakably wooden, the pieces have a weight and mass very uncharacteristic of most contemporary turned vessels.

89

JIM PARTRIDGE

England
B. 1953

Blood Vessel Series
H. 4 1/2" x D. 6 3/4" x W. 9"
Scorched burr oak
1987
95.01.01.174

This piece in Partridge's *Blood Vessel Series* exhibits his exploration of extreme mass and form through the bowl's gentle curvature.

U.S.A.

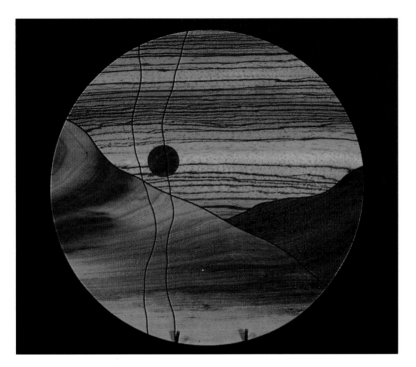

Plate

Diam. 11"
*Zebra wood, mahogany, walnut,
ebony, and amaranth*
1981
Donated by Artist
G95.01.01.175

William Patrick has created a landscape in wood, by cutting and combining four different wood elements with veneer seams. The work was turned in the form of a plate after being assembled.

91

Stephen Paulsen

California, U.S.A.
B. 1947

A Collection of Goblets and Chalices from the Seventeen Peoples of the Eight Inter Worlds

H. 9″ x W. 12″ x D. 3 1/2″
*Wenge, mahogany, buckeye burl, ebony,
kingwood, pink ivory wood, cocobolo,
macadamia, wild lilac burl, African blackwood,
tagua ivory nut, antique ivory, olive wood,
vera wood, O. ivory wood, boxwood,
pernambuco, partridge wood, mazanita, gold*
1987
Donated by Irv Lipton
G95.01.01.178

Pre-Columbian No. 2

D. 1 1/2″ x H. 7″
*Ceonothus burl
and ebony*
1981
*Loaned
anonymously*
L95.01.01.180

In *Pre-Columbian No. 2*, Stephen Paulsen departs from many years of turning scent containers which, although popular, are so uniform in design that they almost seem mass-produced. This piece displays a unique combination of shapes and textures, including both round and square elements. The surface of the lid displays Paulsen's trademark "chatter work." Paulsen fabricates archeological settings for his turned pieces which reflect the cultures of imaginary civilizations.

England
B. 1914　D. 1993

Threaded Lidded Needle Container

L. 7 1/2″ x Diam. 7/8″
Rosewood
c. 1980
95.01.01.187

Lidded Container

H. 4 7/8″ x Top Diam. 3 1/8″
Bottom 1 3/4″
Rosewood
c. 1980
95.01.01.189

David Pye, a turner and carver, is known for his writings on woodworking and craftsmanship. These elegant boxes and containers have hand-threaded lids and textured surfaces.

David Pye

England
B. 1914   D. 1993

Threaded Lidded Container

H. 3 1/16" x Diam. 1 1/4"
Blackwood and unidentified wood
c. 1980
95.01.01.191

David Pye's *Threaded Lidded Container* was meticulously created with a specially designed lathe attachment. The surface texture is similar to the technique employed on his bowls, with each flute individually carved. Pye's texturing adds dimension, light and shadow to the smooth polished surface.

Wayne and Belinda Raab

North Carolina, U.S.A.
B. 1946   B. 1948

Vase: Red with Blue Square
H. 24″ x W. 6 1/2″ x D. 5″
Walnut, curly maple, acrylic lacquer
1987
95.01.01.195

Wayne and Belinda Raab have combined their talents to integrate turning and surface painting in an exquisite piece latent with motion and drama. The painted squares seem to dance up the sides of the vase and drop into a perfectly formed square opening at top.

GAIL REDMAN

California, U.S.A.
B. 1945

Railing with Newel Post
H. 44 1/2″ x W. 5 1/2″ x L. 39 1/4″
Redwood
1983
Donated by Artist
G95.01.01.196

Gail Redman is a production turner who makes wood
architectural embellishments. She was trained by a master
turner and carries on the traditions of spindle and faceplate
turning.

California, U.S.A.
B. 1945

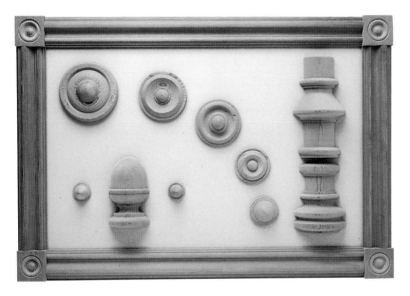

Rosettes and Finials

Diam. 11 1/2″ to 5″
Redwood
1983
Donated by Artist
G95.01.01.197

ALLEN RITZMAN

West Virginia, U.S.A.
B. 1952

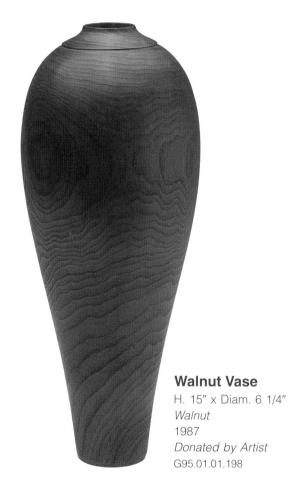

Walnut Vase
H. 15″ x Diam. 6 1/4″
Walnut
1987
Donated by Artist
G95.01.01.198

Allen Ritzman uses a traditionally detailed lip and collar in this hollow vase. The classic proportions of the vase are simply and elegantly expressed in walnut.

California, U.S.A.
B. 1950

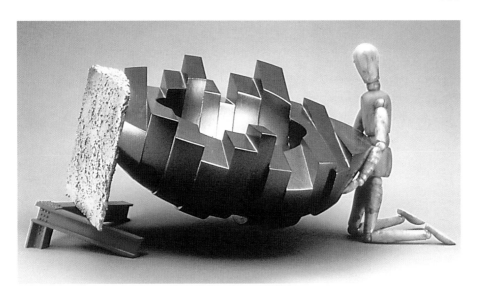

Perfect Reflection
H. 9 1/2" x W. 19" x D. 16"
*Poplar, polyester resin,
acrylic lacquer, artist mannequin*
1986
95.01.01.201

Hap Sakwa has created a tableau, *Perfect Reflection,*
which uses the bowl and a small human figure as a metaphor
for life. Sakwa, the philosopher/turner, has represented his
personal struggle to find balance and harmony in life.

Hap Sakwa

California, U.S.A.
B. 1950

Against That Which All Else Is Measured

H. 17 1/2' x W. 17" x D. 12 1/2"
Poplar, maple, lacquer, violin neck
circa 1780
1985
95.01.01.202

Here, in *Against That Which All Else Is Measured,* Sakwa combines turned, constructed, and one found object (the violin neck), each component representing a measure or standard. This is Sakwa's last in a series of compote turnings with arranged objects.

California, U.S.A.
B. 1950

Space Burger
H. 57″ x Diam. 15″
Poplar, acrylic paint, BB's
1987
Donated by Artist
G95.01.01.203

Sakwa pokes fun at American popular culture with this sculptural hamburger which could serve as a hood or lawn ornament. At nearly five feet, *Space Burger* is one of Sakwa's largest turnings.

ROBERT SALMONSEN

Pennsylvania, U.S.A.
B. 1946

With Pearl Tower
H. 9" x W. 2 1/2" x D. 2 1/2"
Poplar
1987
95.01.01.208

Red Star Hold
H. 11" x W. 2 3/4" x D. 2 3/4"
Apple
1988
95.01.01.205

Robert Salmonsen combines the joy of fantasy with the satisfaction of turning and carving wood. The castles, *Red Star Hold* and *With Pearl Tower,* seem to grow out of carved tree roots. They were turned and carved from single pieces of milled wood.

California, U.S.A.
B. 1949

Box
H. 6 1/2″ x Diam. 1 3/8″
Blackwood and bamboo
1990
Donated by Artist
G95.01.01.210

Jon Sauer is an ornamental turner who is anticipating retirement to fully enjoy his avocation. His work is characteristically ornate with textures created by his mastery of the Holtzapffel lathe. In this box, Sauer strives to combine the richness of the materials with the decorative qualities of the surface treatments.

MERRYLL SAYLAN

California, U.S.A.
B. 1936

North Seas
H. 2 1/4" x Diam. 20 1/2"
Maple with fiber-reactive dye
1987
95.01.01.212

Merryll Saylan uses rich color and texture on a flat turned wood bowl to create this moonscape turning, titled *North Seas*. She is a full-time turner and teacher.

Ohio, U.S.A.
B. 1945

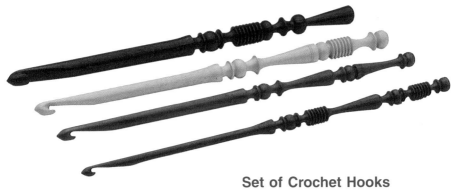

Set of Crochet Hooks
L. 7 1/2″ x Diam. 5/8″ each
Assorted woods
1980
Loaned anonymously
L95.01.01.214

William Schmidt spent years evolving his delicate style of spindle turning. These crochet hooks of various sizes revive the artistry once common in tool making. Schmidt is a full-time production turner specializing in various functional objects of his own design.

TODD HOYER AND BO SCHMITT

U.S.A./Australia
B. 1952   B. 1949

Shapes of Things to Come
Diam. 16″ x L. 16″
Curly ash
1995
Donated by the Artists
G95.09.01.001

Todd Hoyer and Bo Schmitt, both residents in the 1995 International Turning Exchange of the Wood Turning Center, unwittingly collaborated to create this sculpture. Schmitt took Hoyer's experimental turned elements and rearranged them in an allegorical work titled *Shapes of Things to Come.*

Australia
B. 1949

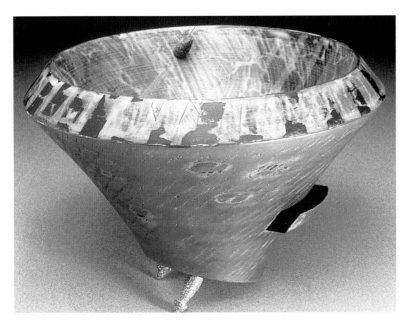

From 'The Dark Heart,'
Book 4, Chapter 7
H. 9 1/4" x Diam. 12 3/4"
MDF, Corian, enamel, acrylic, and bronze
1995, July
Donated by Artist
G95.09.01.003

Bo Schmitt read in Australia about a Philadelphia court case involving a "Move" member and subsequently followed the proceedings during his 1995 International Turning Exchange residency. Disenchanted by the experience, he created *From 'The Dark Heart,' Book 4, Chapter 7,* which thematically addresses the dark side of human nature.

JOHN SCHULZ

California, U.S.A.
B. 1919

Bow!
H. 6 1/2″ x Diam. 10″
Assorted woods
1980
Loaned anonymously
L95.01.01.215

John Schulz creates the appearance of a faceted vessel
through the use of polychromatic turning. The surface of this
polished wood bowl is in reality smooth and round.

108

New Jersey, U.S.A.
B. 1923

Petrified Basket
H. 14" x Diam. 14"
*Wenge, mahogany, sebrawood,
purple heart, poplar, and satinwood*
1987
Donated by Artist
G95.01.01.216

Lincoln Seitzman began turning in his sixties and has found a second and very fulfilling career. His turned and constructed vessels are inspired by southwest Indian basketry. Seitzman arranges the wood by color to create the illusion of texture, light, and shadow as if the vessel were actually woven from reeds.

109

Mark Sfirri

Pennsylvania, U.S.A.
B. 1952

Bat

L. 29 3/4″ x W. 3 1/4″ x D. 2 5/8″
Ash
1994
Donated by Artist
G95.01.01.218

A baseball bat is a simple form that generates memories
of summer, youth, a crowd, and, of course, the game. Mark Sfirri
designed *Bat* for the purpose of presenting this common object
in a different, somewhat disturbing, light.

MARK SFIRRI AND ROBERT DODGE

Pennsylvania, U.S.A.
B. 1952   B. 1939

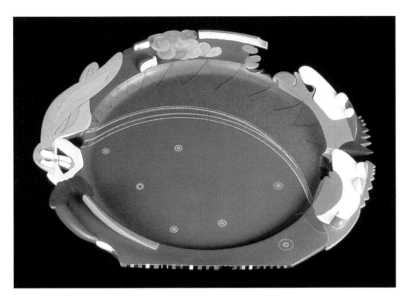

Bugs and Thugs

H. 6" x W. 22 1/2" x D. 25"
Poplar wood, acrylic and gold leaf
Paint and gold leaf by Robert Dodge
1987
Loaned anonymously
L95.01.01.217

Bug and Thugs is a collaborative project by Mark Sfirri and Robert Dodge. Many sketches were made in order to finalize the concept. The turning and carving was done by Sfirri; Dodge painted the imagery.

111

Palmer Sharpless

Pennsylvania, U.S.A.
B. 1922

Honey Dippers
H. 1" x W. 1" x L. 7"
Walnut
1988
Loaned anonymously
L95.01.01.220

Circus
H. 2" x W. 2" x L. 4"
Dogwood
1988
Donated by Artist
G95.01.01.219

Palmer Sharpless, master turner and educator, initially designed honey dippers to be used with his daughter's ceramic honey pots. Having made more than 9,000, they have now become his trademark. Sharpless now uses the dippers to teach and demonstrate turning. He also produces a three-ring circus, a toy for babies and adults alike.

Pennsylvania, U.S.A.
B. 1960

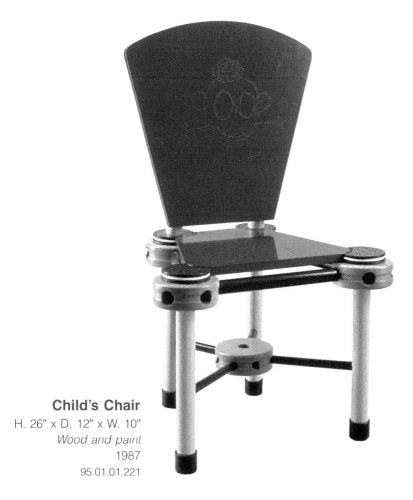

Child's Chair
H. 26" x D. 12" x W. 10"
Wood and paint
1987
95.01.01.221

Joanne Shima made this chair while she was a student of Mark Sfirri's. The chair is designed to be fun for children and has humorous imagery to which they can relate. Images of chocolate cookies with a bite taken out of them provide the function of concealing corners and joints.

MICHAEL SHULER

California, U.S.A.
B. 1950

Cocobolo Bowl #365
H. 5 3/16" x Diam. 11 15/16",
Thickness 119/1000"
Cocobolo
1987
Donated by Artist
G95.01.01.223

Bowl
H. 1 5/8" x Diam. 4 3/4"
Brazilian rosewood
1989
Donated by Artist
G95.01.01.225

Michael Shuler uses a unique polychromatic process which he calls "rearranging." He takes a narrow strip of wood and cuts it into wedges which he then rearranges into different sized rings. Shuler then stacks, laminates and turns the result into thin-walled vessels.

In *Cocobolo Bowl #365,* Shuler uses his "rearranging" process on a more monumental scale.

California, U.S.A.
B. 1950

Pine Cone Bowl
H. 2 1/2″ x Diam. 2 3/8″
*Pine cone and
plastic resin*
1989
95.01.01.224

The unusual surface pattern of this bowl was created by using a pine cone and plastic resin.

TODD HOYER AND HAYLEY SMITH

U.S.A./Wales
B. 1952   B. 1965

Untitled #1
Diam. 16″
Ash
1995
Donated by Artists
G95.09.01.005

Residents in 1995, Todd Hoyer and Hayley Smith personify the collaborative spirit of the International Turning Exchange. This piece was produced collaboratively during the residency. It led to a series of untitled works that they are producing together now, in spite of the fact that they reside on different sides of the pond.

New Mexico, U.S.A.
B. 1952

Bowl
H. 6″ x Diam. 13 1/2″
Wood, lacquered and gold leaf
1985
Loaned anonymously
L95.01.01.226

Robert Sterba is a furniture maker and turner. He uses layered lacquer and hammered gold leaf on this richly colored vessel.

117

ALAN STIRT

Vermont, U.S.A.
B. 1946

Fluted Bowl
H. 7" x Diam. 20"
Butternut
1985
Loaned anonymously
L95.01.01.228

Alan Stirt is known for his functional, textured vessels. This bowl is one of his largest fluted creations and represents a marked departure in style and workmanship. Stirt's early work was planned with mathematical precision. Beginning with this piece, he has achieved more freedom and expression.

Vermont, U.S.A.
B. 1946

War Bowl
H. 5 3/4" x Diam. 9"
Ceanothus burl
1990
95.01.01.230

Stirt usually strives for beauty and a sense of peace in his work. His bowls can be seen as symbols of wholeness, but *War Bowl* is a wounded bowl. Created just after the Gulf War, it is a statement about war and its effect on the human spirit. This piece marks an embarkation for an artistic realm which Stirt continues to explore.

119

Bob Stocksdale

California, U.S.A.
B. 1913

Yoke Wood Bowl
H. 4 1/2" x Diam. 7 1/4"
Yoke wood (Africa)
1979
Loaned anonymously
L95.01.01.234

African Blackwood Bowl
H. 2" x Diam. 6 3/4"
African blackwood
1977
Loaned anonymously
L95.01.01.235

Bob Stocksdale is a master of the classic bowl form. He was among the first artists to use exotic imported woods in decorative bowls. The *Yoke Wood Bowl* developed from the natural elliptical curvature of the log. In profile it resembles a baby bird's wide-open beak, waiting for a worm.

The *African Blackwood Bowl* combines several different surface treatments. The rough exterior contrasts with a smooth interior. The vertically textured rim unites the various effects in this Stocksdale anomaly.

California, U.S.A.
B. 1913

Macadamia Wood Bowl
H. 3 1/4" x Diam. 4 3/8"
Macadamia wood
1987
95.01.01.236

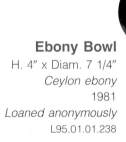

Curly Ash Wood Bowl
H. 3" x Diam. 11"
Curly ash wood (English ash)
1987
95.01.01.237

Ebony Bowl
H. 4" x Diam. 7 1/4"
Ceylon ebony
1981
Loaned anonymously
L95.01.01.238

Stocksdale creates a painting in wood with each of his pieces. *Macadamia Wood Bowl* depicts a sunburst and *Ebony Bowl* represents a canyon landscape. The uniform wall thickness of these pieces is abandoned in *Curly Ash Wood Bowl*. Stocksdale breaks with his usual style and adds a wider lip with a thicker rim.

Timothy Stokes

Great Britain
B. 1964

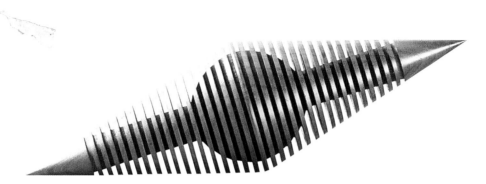

Double Cone/Sphere
L. 14 1/2″ x Diam. 4 1/2″
Black walnut
1995, July
Donated by Artist
G95.09.01.004

Timothy Stokes, during his 1995 International Turning Exchange residency, created *Double Cone/Sphere,* a paradoxical form within a form. This is a unique turned walnut object that symbolizes duality of inner and outer existence.

Hawaii, U.S.A.
B. 1934

Koa Bowl
H. 6" x Diam. 10 3/4"
Koa
c. 1979
Loaned anonymously
L95.01.01.241

Jack Straka works with Hawaiian-grown woods and has successfully turned over fifty species. Most of his work is made from koa—a dramatically grained Hawaiian wood. This *Koa Bowl,* circa 1979, is a classical example of Jack Straka's turning work and contains the patching of cracks characteristic of repairs to traditional calabash bowls.

ROBERT STREET

Washington, U.S.A.
B. 1919

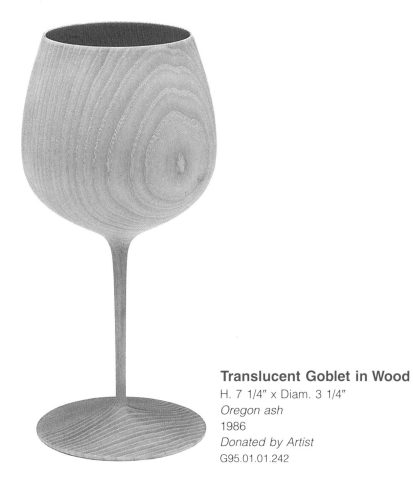

Translucent Goblet in Wood
H. 7 1/4″ x Diam. 3 1/4″
Oregon ash
1986
Donated by Artist
G95.01.01.242

Robert Street is an architect by training and turner by choice. *Translucent Goblet in Wood* is so masterfully designed and executed that it would be nearly impossible for him to duplicate.

DEL STUBBS

Minnesota, U.S.A.
B. 1952

Bowl
H. 2 3/4″ x Diam. 11 1/4″
Olive
1980
Donated by Artist
G95.01.01.243

Translucent Bowl
H. 1 7/8″ x Diam. 4 1/2″
Curly maple
1979
Donated by Artist
G95.01.01.245

Del Stubbs, a master of a variety of woodworking processes, achieves an unmatchable delicacy in his turning. Stubbs has pioneered the art of translucent turning.

Del Stubbs

Minnesota, U.S.A.
B. 1952

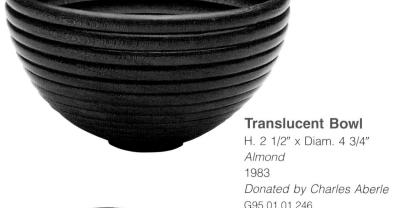

Translucent Bowl
H. 2 1/2″ x Diam. 4 3/4″
Almond
1983
Donated by Charles Aberle
G95.01.01.246

Container
H. 2 1/8″ x Diam. 3 3/8″
Myrtle
1980
Loaned anonymously
L95.01.01.250

Stubbs's work in turning suggests the coils of pottery but is masterfully produced in wood. He has also revived the art of box making. This container has a lid and body made from one piece of wood. It displays a book-match inlaid lid.

China

Chinese Balls
H. 7" x Diam. 2 7/8"
Ivory
Loaned anonymously
L95.01.01.254

This ornately turned and carved ivory object consists of balls inside of balls on a pedestal. It is an exquisite and classic example of an ancient Asian decorative art.

Maria van Kesteren

Netherlands
B. 1933

Volume
H. 3 1/8″ x Diam. 10 1/8″
Elm and gray paint
1982
95.01.01.257

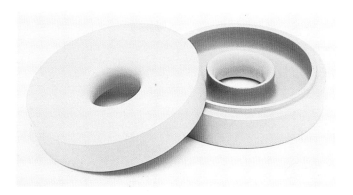

Box
H. 2″ x Diam. 5 1/8″
Elm and gray paint
1984
95.01.01.258

Maria van Kesteren pioneered the use of color on lathe-turned objects. She designs and executes pure forms as seen in this vessel and box. Van Kesteren explores the radial symmetry of circular forms and employs color to downplay the grain in the wood.

Netherlands
B. 1933

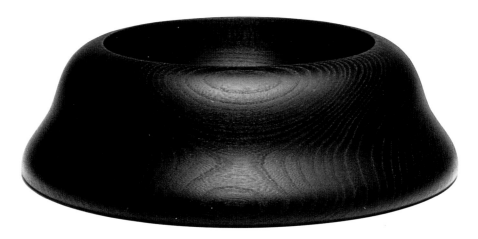

Landscape
H. 3 1/2" x Diam. 12 1/8"
Elm and indigo paint
1987
95.01.01.259

Landscape is uncharacteristic in its acceptance of the grain of the wood as part of the artistic statement.

Jay Weber

Pennsylvania, U.S.A.
B. 1919

Wing Nut with Screw
W. 4 5/8" x D. 4 3/8"
Maple
1995
96.10.23.002

Oil Can
H. 6 3/4" x Diam. 3 1/8"
Cherry
1989
Loaned anonymously
L95.01.01.261

Jay Weber, a full-time production turner, learned from and was influenced by the Brubakers. *Oil Can* is typical of the whimsical nonfunctional objects he produces. His work clearly takes pleasure in turning for turning's sake.

Pennsylvania, U.S.A.
B. 1919

Wedding Cups
each H. 4 3/4" x Diam. 3 3/8"
Cherry
1993
Loaned anonymously
L96.10.20.001a.b.

The Brubaker influence is apparent in Jay Weber's lidded container. Weber has adapted the Brubaker signature form, the saffron container, to serve as a symbolic wedding cup. Over the stem of the turned wood cup there are two wood rings that cannot be removed. Although they rotate freely, they also rest flush in a niche in the base. Weber says these rings symbolize a happily married couple because they are close together and compatible, but yet free and separate individuals.

CHRISTOPHER WEILAND

Pennsylvania, U.S.A.
B. 1950

Wall Mirror
H. 3″ x Diam. 15″
Maple, paint, brass
1987
95.01.01.264

Christopher Weiland, a professor of woodworking at Indiana University in Pennsylvania, designs and makes functional and sculptural objects. This folding hand mirror is both useful and decorative.

Germany
B. 1954

Ball-Box, Turned Broken Through
Diam. 2″
African blackwood and boxwood
1992
Donated by Irv Lipton
G95.01.01.270

Ball-Box, Turned Broken Through With Windows
Diam. 2″
Boxwood
1992
Donated by Irv Lipton
G95.01.01.274

Hans Joachim Weissflog was a student of Professor Gottfried Bockelmann. *Ball-Box, Turned Broken Through* was a major breakthrough for Weissflog, allowing him to find his own artistic voice. This piece has become an award-winning signature piece.

He explores a variation of the theme in *Ball-Box, Turned Broken Through With Windows*. It has one-piece construction, which is a great technical challenge.

Hans Joachim Weissflog

Germany
B. 1954

Saturn Box
H. 2″ x W. 4 3/4″ x D. 4 3/4″
Boxwood burl
1992
Donated by Irv Lipton
G95.01.01.269

Saturn Box, consisting of a ball-box in the middle and a disk with a natural edge, is made from one piece of wood. In order to show the complete burl, Weissflog determined it was necessary to leave the natural edge on the outside.

Germany
B. 1954

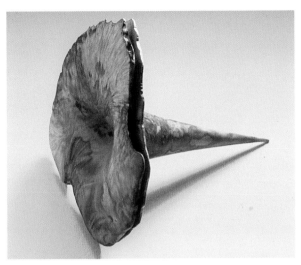

Box Blossom

H. 4″ x W. 4 3/8″ x D. 5″
Boxwood burl
1992
*Promised gift
by Eileen Silver*
G95.03.13.001

135

Germany
B. 1954

**Bowl, Turned Broken
Through; Spider Bowl**
Diam. 8″
Yew wood
1994
Donated by Artist
G95.01.01.273

Spider Bowl is a departure from Weissflog's work with boxes. He wanted to capture the viewer's attention with this larger than usual turning. It is also unique in that it is one of his first open-form vessels.

Australia
B. 1939

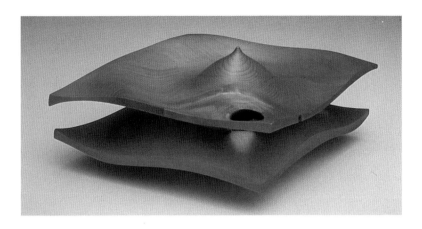

Huon Pine Box
H. 2 1/2" x D. 4" x W. 5"
Huon pine
1987
95.01.01.276

Bowl
H. 6" x W. 22 1/2" x D. 14"
Red gum
1987
Donated by Artist
G96.04.09.002

Vic Wood was instrumental in the development and promotion of the art of wood turning in Australia. He employs an unparalleled process where he turns lidded containers within rectangular shapes.

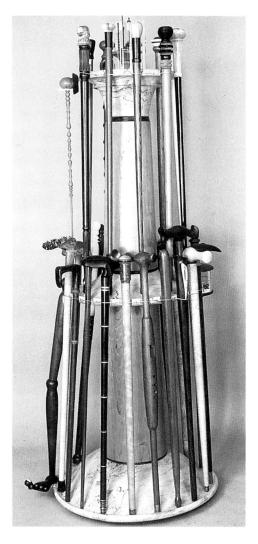

Collection of Canes
H. 68" x Diam. 24"
Various materials
1989
Loaned by Albert and Tina LeCoff
L95.01.01.003.a-.dd

Coordinated by Wendy and Johannes Michelsen, lathe-turners from around the world contributed handmade canes to present to Albert LeCoff in appreciation for his advancement of turning among the arts. "Albert helped us walk from the craft field to the arts," they said when they presented their gift.

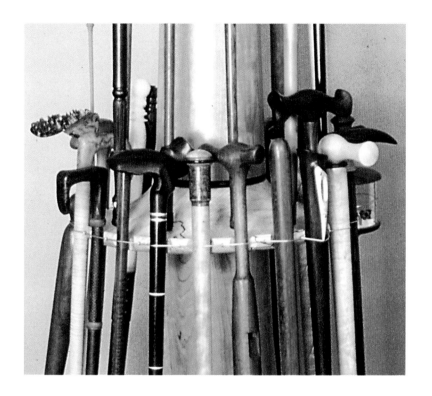

Roger Barnes
Ed Bosley
Rod Cronkite
Frank E. Cummings, III
Walter Dexter
Leo Doyle
Dennis Elliott
David Ellsworth
Giles Gilson
Michelle Holzapfel
Todd Hoyer
C.R. "Skip" Johnson
John Jordan
Bonnie Klein
Frank Knox

"R.W." Bob Krauss
Andreas Kutsche
Dan Kvitka
Steve Loar
Johannes Michelsen
Bruce Mitchell
Michael Mode
Stephen Paulsen
Michael Peterson
Richard Raffan
Bob Sonday
Ric Stang
Bob Stocksdale
Del Stubbs
Christopher Weiland

LIST OF COLLECTION

Objects in the Wood Turning Center's collections not pictured in this book.

Françios Achilli
Pen, 1995
Various woods
L. 6" x Diam. 5/8"
L96.04.09.001

Ray Allen
Vessel, 1996
Various woods
H. 9" x Diam. 8"
G96.11.16.007
Gift of Irv Lipton

Bruce Bernson
Putter, 1996
Various woods, Corian, metal
L. 36"
G96.11.16.006
Gift of Irv Lipton

Gottfried Bockelmann
Cross-Turned Globe Box,
1987
Acacia (false)
Diam. 3 1/4"
G95.01.01.004
Gift of the artist

Ribbed Jar, 1987
Boxwood
H. 5 7/8" x Diam. 2 7/8"
95.01.01.005

Michael Brolly
Dancing Tryclops, 1996
H. 22" x D. 18" x W. 19 1/2"
Curly maple and dyed
veneer
G96.11.16.001
Gift of the artist

Shark Bowl, 1981
Koa
H. 1 3/4" x Diam. 5 1/4"
95.01.01.008

Jake Brubaker
Rolling Pin, c. 1978
Bubinga, rosewood, pewter
L. 19 1/2" x Diam. 3"
L95.01.01.012

Small Cup, 1977
Plastic
H. 2" x Diam. 1 1/2"
L95.01.01.013

Cup, 1975
Rosewood
H. 6" x Diam. 1 1/2"
L95.01.01.014

M. Dale Chase
Lidded Container, 1987
African blackwood
H. 2 7/8" x D. 3 1/8" x
W. 3 1/8"
95.01.01.020

Lidded Container, 1980
African blackwood and silver
H. 2 3/8" x Diam. 1 1/2"
L95.01.01.019

Lidded Container, c. 1988
Lignum vitae
H. 3" x Diam. 2 1/2"
L95.01.01.024

Lidded Container, c. 1988
Honduras rosewood and
African blackwood inlay
H. 2 3/4" x Diam. 2 1/2"
L95.01.01.025

Lidded Containers, c. 1988
Lignum vitae
H. 3" x Diam. 2 3/4"
L95.01.01.026

Lidded Container, c. 1988
African blackwood
H. 2 3/4" x Diam. 3 1/8"
L95.01.01.027

**Peter Chatwin &
Pamela Martin**
Stud Earrings, c. 1987
Laminated sycamore veneer
Diam. 1 7/8"
L95.01.01.028a.b

Karl Decker
Spinning Top, 1987
Ebony, rosewood
H. 1 5/8" x Diam. 1 1/8"
95.01.01.037

John Diamond-Nigh
Untitled, c. 1985
Birch
H. 7 1/4" x Diam. 8"
95.01.01.039

Wing Form, 1987
Birch
H. 3" x L. 30" x W. 3 1/2"
95.01.01.041

East German
German Nutcracker
Wood and paint
H. 14 1/2" x W. 4 1/2" x
D. 3"
L95.01.01.102b

David Ellsworth
Vessel, 1979
Bubinga
Diam. 7 1/2" x H. 2 3/4"
L95.01.01.049

Vase, 1982
Box elder
H. 9" x Diam. 3"
L95.01.01.052

Vessel, 1978
Figured walnut
H. 2" x Diam. 10"
L95.01.01.053

Jean-François Escoulen
La Metamorphose, 1996
Oak burl, Chekanakot,
ebony
H. 11" x D. 6 1/4" x L. 18"
G96.11.16.008
Gift of the artist

**Jean-François Escoulen/
Mark Sfirri**
Hurdy Gurdy, 1996
Wood and paint
H. 17" x W. 4 1/2" x
D. 4 1/2"
L96.11.16.002

Paul Eshelman
Platter, 1977
Oak
H. 1 1/2" x Diam. 15 3/8"
L95.01.01.055

J. Paul Fennell
Miniature Goblets #1, 1987
Rosewood and ebony series
From H. 1/8" to 1 1/4"
G95.01.01.056
Gift of the artist

140

LIST OF COLLECTION

Miniature Goblets #2, 1987
Boxwood series
From H. 3/4" to 1 5/8"
G95.01.01.057
Gift of the artist

Stephan Fink
Pencil, 1989
Ebony
L. 6" x Diam. 5/8"
L95.01.01.059

Doug Finkel
Mallet, 1996
Various woods
L. 9 1/2" x W. 5 1/2" x D. 3"
G96.11.16.005
Gift of the artist

Ron Fleming
Crocus, 1996
Redwood burl
H. 2" x Diam. 3 1/2"
L96.10.23.003

German Library
Flower Seller, 1989
Various woods and paint
H. 4" x W. 4" x D. 5"
L95.01.01.061a-h

Giles Gilson
Bowl, 1985
Mahogany; pearlescent
lacquer
H. 4 1/4" x Diam. 7"
95.01.01.062

Vessel, 1993
Wood and paint
H. 13" x Diam. 5 1/4"
G96.11.16.009
Gift of Irv Lipton

John Grass Company
Billy Club, c. 1970
Oak
L. 12" x Diam. 1 5/8"
G95.01.01.069
Gift from the Company

Bundle of Balusters, c. 1970
Various woods and sizes
G95.01.01.070
Gift from the Company

Finial, c. 1970
Redwood
L. 10" x Diam. 5"
G95.01.01.071
Gift from the Company

Foundry mallet, c. 1970
Cherry
L. 10 3/8" x Diam. 2 5/8"
G95.01.01.072
Gift from the Company

Large Mallet, c. 1970
Ash
L. 36 2/3" x Diam. 5 5/8"
G95.01.01.073
Gift from the Company

Offering Plate, c. 1970
Walnut
H. 1 5/8" x Diam. 12"
G95.01.01.074
Gift from the Company

Rolling Pin, c. 1970
Poplar
L. 18 1/2" x Diam. 2 1/2"
G95.01.01.075
Gift from the Company

Rolling Pin, c. 1970
Cherry
L. 27 1/2" x Diam. 4"
G95.01.01.076
Gift from the Company

Small Mallet, c. 1970
Cherry
L. 10 3/8" x Diam. 2 5/8"
G95.01.01.077
Gift from the Company

Stephen Hogbin
Spoons, c. 1978
Birch
L. 15 3/4" x W. 1 3/4"
L95.01.01.083a.b

Michelle Holzapfel
Vessel, 1980
Wild cherry burl
H. 4 1/4" x Diam. 6 15/16"
L95.01.01.084

Michael Hosaluk
Mach IV, 1986
Colorcore, anodized
aluminum, glass, lacquered
maple
H. 24" x Diam. 18 1/2"
95.01.01.089

Lynne Hull
Strapped Bowl Form #2,
1992
Aluminum
H. 2 3/4" x D. 9 1/2" x
W. 11 1/2"
95.01.01.096

Black Tie Affair, 1986
Aluminum, lacquer paints
H. 4" x Diam. 14"
L95.01.01.094

Basket #2, 1983
Painted aluminum, plastic
H. 11 3/4" x Diam. 7 3/4"
L95.01.01.095

William Hunter
Flutes for Albert, 1985
Cocobolo
H. 5" x Diam. 6 1/4"
L95.01.01.099

Italian
Doll
Wood and paint
H. 15 1/2" x W. 4 1/4" x
D. 3 1/2"
L95.01.01.102a

C.R. "Skip" Johnson
Fake Box, 1981
Bubinga
H. 6 5/8" x W. 3 1/8" x
D. 3 3/4"
G95.01.01.106
Gift of the artist

Tom Kealy
2 Somerset Sidechairs &
1 Arm Somerset Sidechair,
1987
Ash and willow
each H. 39" x W. 18" x
D. 19"
95.01.01.109a.b.
95.01.01.108

Richard Kell
Three Tray Box, 1987
Anodized aluminum, maple
H. 4" x Diam. 2"
L95.01.01.111

Don Kelly
Horizon Bowl, 1988
Maple, aluminum base
H. 15 1/2" x W. 23" x
D. 4 1/2"
95.01.01.112

Wild Cherry Burl, c. 1979
Cherry burl, epoxy and baby
powder
H. 3 1/4" x Diam. 5 3/4"
L95.01.01.113

"R.W." Bob Krauss
Lidded Vessel, 1986
Chittam burl
H. 4 1/4" x Diam. 3 1/2"
L95.01.01.122

Max Krimmel
Alabaster Bowl #196,
c. 1987
Alabaster and wood
H. 4 1/2" x Diam. 17"
G95.01.01.125
Gift of the artist

Leon Lacoursiere
Vessel, c. 1988
Wood
H. 7" x W. 6 7/16" x
D. 3 9/16"
95.01.01.126

Stoney Lamar
Torso Reclining, 1987
Walnut
H. 26" x W. 19" x D. 4 3/4"
G96.11.25.001
Gift of Fleur Bresler

Bud Latven
Irv's Grief, 1994
Various woods
H. 25" x W. 29" x D. 7"
G95.06.01.001
Gift of the artist and Irv
Lipton

Wenge Bowl, 1987
Wenge and holly
H. 4 1/4" x Diam. 3 3/4"
L95.01.01.128

Bloodwood Bowl, 1987
Bloodwood, ebony, holly
H. 4" x Diam. 3 1/2"
L95.01.01.129

Mel Lindquist
Vessel, 1980
Maple
H. 4 11/16 x Diam. 3"
G95.01.01.133
Gift of Rick and Ruth
Snyderman

Terry Martin
Vessel, 1996
Maple burl
H. 9" x W. 15" x D. 10 1/2"
G96.11.16.003
Gift of the artist

Hugh McKay
Blue Rose, 1996
Rosewood and glass
H. 9 1/2" x Diam. 9 1/2"
G96.11.16.004
Gift of the artist

John Megin
Bowl, 1980
Sugar maple
H. 3 1/4" x Diam. 10 5/8"
G95.01.01.145
Gift of Arthur and Mary Megin

Bowl, 1984
Green ash
H. 2 1/2" x Diam. 5 5/8"
G95.01.01.146
Gift of Arthur and Mary Megin

Bowl, 1985
American hornbean
H. 2 3/4" x Diam. 4 5/8"
G95.01.01.147
Gift of Arthur and Mary Megin

Johannes Michelsen
Hat, 1993
Maple
H. 5" x Diam. 15"
L95.01.01.149

Michael Mode
Ornaments, c. 1988
Poplar and paint
each L. 5" x Diam. 1 1/2"
95.01.01.153a.b.c.d.

Liz/Michael O'Donnell
Bowl, 1985
Plum
H. 2 1/4' x Diam. 7"
L95.01.01.161

Liam O'Neill
Walnut Functional Bowl,
1985
European walnut
H. 3 1/4" x Diam. 10"
L95.01.01.162

Rude Osolnik
Bowl, 1966
Maple impregnated with
colored plastic through
irradiation
H. 1 7/8" x W. 9 1/4" x
D. 9 5/8"
L95.01.01.168

Natural Top Bowl, 1977
Walnut spurr
H. 3 1/4" x Diam. 8 3/4"
L95.01.01.169

Jim Partridge
Blood Vessel Series, 1987
Scorched burr oak
H. 6" x Diam. 7 1/4"
95.01.01.172

Blood Vessel Series, 1987
Scorched burr oak
H. 5" x L. 11 3/4" x
D. 8 3/4"
95.01.01.173

Stephen Paulsen
Stopper Container, 1985
Blackwood, macassar ebony
H. 2 1/2" x Diam. 3/4"
L95.01.01.176

Blackwood Box, 1987
Blackwood
H. 2" x Diam. 1 1/2"
L95.01.01.177

Stopper container, 1985
Blackwood, rosewood
H. 3 1/2" x Diam. 1"
L95.01.01.179

Gord Peteran
Untitled, 1996
Stitched leather and wood
L. 20" x W. 7" x D. 7"
L96.11.20.001

David Pye
Lidded Container, c. 1980
Rosewood
H. 3 3/4" x Diam. 2 1/4"
95.01.01.184

Lidded Container, c. 1980
Unidentified wood
H. 2 1/2" x Diam. 2 3/8"
95.01.01.186

Box, c. 1980
Macassar ebony
H. 1 1/2" x Diam. 3 1/4"
95.01.01.188

Threaded Lidded Container,
c. 1980
Blackwood
H. 1 1/2" x Diam. 2 1/4"
95.01.01.190

Quelle Est Belle Company
Bird Whistles, c. 1990
Various woods and metals
From L. 3 1/8″ to 4 5/8″
G95.01.01.060a-l
Gift of Hans Weissflog

Hap Sakwa
Malibu, 1986
Poplar wood, acrylics,
acrylic lacquer
H. 4 1/2″ x Diam. 15 ″
95.01.01.200

Robert Salmonsen
Small Castle, c. 1988
Apple
H. 5″ x W. 2″ x D. 2″
95.01.01.204

Castle, 1989
Paint and apple
H. 6 1/2″ x Diam. 2″
95.01.01.206

Castle, 1989
Paint and apple
H. 6 1/2″ x W. 2″ x D. 2″
95.01.01.207

Castle, c. 1988
Paint and apple
H. 9 1/2″ x Diam. 2″
95.01.01.209

Norm Sartorius
Spoon with Base, 1986
Quilted Honduras mahogany,
rose of the mountain, and
ebony
H. 1 1/2″ x W. 3/2″ x L. 16″
G96.10.23.001a.b
Gift of Fleur Bresler

Jon Sauer
Blackwood Container, 1993
Blackwood
H. 5 1/2″ x Diam. 1 1/2″
95.01.01.211

Henry Schaefer
Honey Dippers, 1981
Maple, ebony
each L. 8″
95.01.01.213a.b.c.d.e

Joanne Shima
Child's Chair, 1987
Maple, birch, medium-
density fiberboard, lacquer
H. 21″ x W. 14″ x D. 12″
95.01.01.222

Alan Stirt
Textured Bowl, 1987
Cocobolo
H. 4 1/8″ x Diam. 10″
95.01.01.227

Fluted Bowl, 1981
Cocobolo
H. 4″ x Diam. 9 1/2″
L95.01.01.229

Bob Stocksdale
Putumuju Wood Bowl, 1985
Putumuju wood
H. 3 3/4″ x Diam. 8″
95.01.01.232

Snakewood Bowl, 1988
Snakewood
H. 5 1/2″ x Diam. 6″
G95.01.01.231
Gift of Charles Aberle

Plate, c. 1976
Goncalo alves
H. 1 3/4″ x Diam. 11 1/2″
L95.01.01.233

Kingwood Bowl, 1990
Kingwood
H. 2 3/8″ x Diam. 4 3/4″
L95.01.01.239

Jack Straka
Koa Bowl, c. 1979
Koa
H. 9″ x Diam. 5 1/2″
L95.01.01.240

Del Stubbs
Container, 1981
Clara walnut
Diam. 5 1/2″ x H. 3 1/2″
95.01.01.244

Clara Walnut Vase, 1980
Clara walnut
H. 8 1/2″ x Diam. 2 1/2″
L95.01.01.242

Top, c. 1980
Maple
H. 1 1/2″ x Diam. 1 1/2″
L95.01.01.253

Top, c. 1980
Maple and walnut
H. 1 1/2″ x Diam. 1 1/2″
L95.01.01.247

Container, 1980
Apricot
H. 2 3/4″ x Diam. 3 1/2″
L95.01.01.248

Container, 1980
Walnut, curly maple
H. 2 3/16″ x Diam. 3 3/8″
L95.01.01.249

Container, 1980
Clara walnut and olive
H. 2 1/8″ x Diam. 3 3/8″
L95.01.01.251

Container, 1982
Clara walnut and black
locust
H. 1 7/8″ x Diam. 3 7/8″
L95.01.01.252

Maria van Kesteren
Box, 1996
Elm and paint
H. 2 1/2″ x Diam. 6 7/8″
L96.10.23.004

Jay Weber
Goblet, 1981
Rosewood
H. 1 15/16″ x Diam. 3/4″
L95.01.01.263

Wing Nut With Screw, 1987
Cherry
H. 2 7/8″ x W. 4 5/8″ x
L. 4 3/4″
L95.01.01.260

Hans Joachim Weissflog
Napoleon Box, 1992
Purpleheart
H. 2″ x W. 2 3/4″ x
D. 1 1/2″
G95.01.01.265
Gift of Irv Lipton

Round Box, 1992
Burr wood and ebony
H. 1 3/4″ x Diam. 1 3/4″
G95.01.01.268
Gift of Irv Lipton

Walnut Box, 1992
Nut and walnut
H. 1 7/8″ x W. 1 1/2″ x L. 2″
95.01.01.271

Box with Floating Rings,
1992
Blackwood
H. 1 1/4″ x Diam. 1 3/4″
G95.01.01.266
Gift of Irv Lipton

Eiffeltower, 1992
Basswood, ebony
H. 1 1/2″ x Diam. 2″
G95.01.01.275
Gift of Irv Lipton

BY WAY OF THE COLOPHON

This limited edition of *Enter the World of Lathe-Turned Objects* is privately published by York Graphic Services, Inc., of York, Pennsylvania, for the enjoyment of our clients, friends, and associates. An additional number of this printing is being distributed through the Wood Turning Center.

This is the 26th in a series of keepsake books designed by Ray Chronister and produced under his direction by associates of our ESOP company.

The production of this book is completely electronic, with the manuscript supplied to us on floppy disks. These text files were then imported to our Quark Department where pages were produced using QuarkXPress®. The typeface is 10 on 13 Helvetica Roman for the text. All photographs were 35mm, which were scanned on the Scitex 720 Smart Scan and Screen 608 drum scanner. High-resolution color proofs were made on the Iris Ink Jet proofer for color evaluation. Color enhancements and silhouettes were made on the Quadra 900 using Adobe Photoshop®. Iris Ink Jet color proofs with high-resolution images were used for the first page proofs. Final film was output on the Avantra 44 as sixteen-up imposed film using picture replacement for the low-resolution FPOs. Sixteen-up Pressmatch proofs were made for final approval and press match.

This edition was printed using four-color process, at 175 line screen, plus PMS 463 and PMS 468 for the fifth and sixth colors. A spot varnish coating was added to all pictures and the cover was flood coated with aqueous coating. The paper is Consolidated Paper, Inc., 100 lb. Centura Dull Plus Text, a recycled paper. The printing was done on our 40" Heidelberg Speedmaster six-color press by PrintTech, a division of York Graphic Services, Inc., at 3600 West Market Street, York, Pennsylvania 17404.

All for the joy of doing.